# Skills Builders

**YEAR 6**

**SPELLING AND VOCABULARY**

**Sarah Turner**

# Acknowledgements

Every effort has been made to trace all copyright holders, but if any have been inadvertently overlooked, the Publishers will be pleased to make the necessary arrangements at the first opportunity.

Although every effort has been made to ensure that website addresses are correct at time of going to press, Rising Stars cannot be held responsible for the content of any website mentioned in this book. It is sometimes possible to find a relocated web page by typing in the address of the home page for a website in the URL window of your browser.

Hachette UK's policy is to use papers that are natural, renewable and recyclable products and made from wood grown in sustainable forests. The logging and manufacturing processes are expected to conform to the environmental regulations of the country of origin.

ISBN: 978-1-78339-733-4

Text, design and layout © 2019 Hodder & Stoughton Ltd. (for its Rising Stars imprint)

First published in 2016 by Rising Stars, part of Hodder & Stoughton Ltd.
An Hachette UK Company
Carmelite House 50 Victoria Embankment
London EC4Y 0DZ

www.risingstars-uk.com

Reprinted in 2016, 2019, 2020.

All facts are correct at time of going to press.

Author: Sarah Turner
Educational Consultant: Madeleine Barnes
Publisher: Laura White
Illustrator: Emily Skinner
Logo design: Amparo Barrera, Kneath Associates Ltd
Design: Julie Martin
Typesetting: Newgen
Cover design: Amparo Barrera, Kneath Associates Ltd
Project Manager: Seonaid Loader, Out of House Publishing
Copy Editor: Claire Pearce-Jones
Proofreader: Jennie Clifford
Software development: Alex Morris

British Library Cataloguing–in–Publication Data
A CIP record for this book is available from the British Library.
Printed in Slovenia

# Contents

## SPELLING

## VOCABULARY

All of the answers can be found online. To get access, simply register or login
at **www.risingstars-uk.com.**

# 1 Words ending in tious and cious

The **suffixes tious** and **cious** are both used to form adjectives from nouns, and both have a *shus* sound. The noun usually suggests the spelling of the adjective.

| Noun | tious adjective | Noun | cious adjective |
|------|-----------------|------|-----------------|
| ambition | ambitious | price | precious |
| fiction | fictitious | grace | gracious |
| infection | infectious | malice | malicious |
| nutrition | nutritious | delicacy | delicious |

## Activity 1

Use a word from the list to complete each of the sentences below.

vicious    precious    conscious    delicious    malicious    suspicious

ambitious    cautious    fictitious    infectious    nutritious

a) There was a __malicious__ bulge in the thief's pocket.

b) Drivers should be __cautious__ when approaching the bend.

c) The ring was set with __precious__ stones.

d) The dog was __vicious__.

e) The characters in this film are purely __fictitious__.

f) He was put into jail for
   his __suspicious__ behaviour.

g) Isaac made a __delicious__ curry
   for his family.

h) Jade's chickenpox was __infectious__.

i) She was __conscious__ of what she
   said to her mother.

j) Sita took a __nutritious__ snack to have at break time.

k) The company set some very __ambitious__ goals for the year.

## Activity 2

Read the clues and work out the **tious** and **cious** words. Use a dictionary to help if you need to.

**a)** If something is _____ to you, you care about it a lot.

**b)** If you are _____ of something, you think about it.

**c)** If you are _____, you want to achieve a lot.

**d)** Something which is imaginary, and exists only in a storybook is _____.

**e)** An alligator is a _____ animal.

**f)** To be _____ means to think that you are important.

**g)** Someone who is deliberately spiteful and intends to harm is _____.

**h)** If someone is _____, he or she is argumentative.

## Activity 3

Solve these anagrams to work out the words ending with **tious** or **cious**.

ice pours = precious

**a)** a music oil = _____

**b)** sivic ou = _____

**c)** a cut i ous = _____

**d)** i sic outfit = _____

**e)** use coin fit = _____

**f)** pic is sou us = _____

**g)** cosuperi = _____

**h)** sicouiled = _____

**i)** ttnuirsiou = _____

**j)** soitbimau = _____

## Investigate!

How many different words can you find from your reading books, and other books in the school library, with the suffixes **tious** or **cious**? Write a list of the words you find.

# 2 Words ending in cial and tial

The suffixes **cial** and **tial**, which are used to form adjectives, sound like *shul*, but how can you decide which of the two possible spellings to use? It can help to go back to the noun, but not always.

| Noun | cial ending |
| --- | --- |
| face | facial |
| glacier | glacial |
| office | official |
| finance | financial |
| society | social |
| benefit | beneficial |

The link for **tial** is less clear.

| Noun | tial ending |
| --- | --- |
| part | partial, impartial |
| confidence | confidential |
| essence | essential |
| palace | palatial |
| credence | credential |

- If the letter before the suffix is a vowel, it ends in **cial**.
- If the letter before the suffix is a consonant, it ends in **tial**.

**Make sure you check in your dictionary!**

## Activity 1

Add **cial** or **tial** to complete each of these words.

a) residen_tial_

b) espe_____ly

c) offi_____

d) finan_____

e) influen_____

f) commer_____

g) unso_____

h) fa_____

i) inconsequen_____

j) ini_____

Choose four of these words and write a sentence using each one.

## Activity 2

Solve these anagrams to work out the words ending with **cial** or **tial**.

**a)** tail in i = _____

**b)** set aliens = _____

**c)** fair italic = _____

**d)** micro camel = _____

**e)** can nail if = _____

**f)** fail foci = _____

## Activity 3

Copy the table into your book. Use the nouns as root words to create adjectives with the *shul* sound ending. Remember it is spelled either **cial** or **tial**.

| Root word | *shul* **word – cial or tial** |
| --- | --- |
| benefit | |
| society | |
| palace | |
| race | |
| confidence | |
| glacier | |
| province | |
| influence | |
| circumstance | |

## Investigate!

Write a set of rules to explain when to add **tial** or **cial** to a noun.
How many different words with **tial** and **cial** suffixes can you find in your favourite book?

# 3 Words ending in able and ible

Most adjectives with the *able* sound are spelled **able**, and have related verbs and nouns.

| Verb | Adjective | Noun |
|------|-----------|------|
| adore | adorable | adoration |
| apply | applicable | application |
| consider | considerable | consideration |
| reason | reasonable | reasoning |

As the suffix **able** starts with a vowel, you have to check the spelling.

- After a short vowel sound with a single consonant, double the last consonant.
  forget = forgettable

- Drop the final **e**, except after soft consonants such as **g** and **c**.
  change = changeable

- Change a **y** after a consonant to **i**.
  apply = applicable

There are fewer adjectives ending in **ible**, and they have less obvious roots.

**possible, sensible, credible, visible, horrible, terrible**

## Activity 1

Copy the table into your book. Using the spelling rules above, decide whether to add the suffix **able** or **ible** to each word to form adjectives and write the words.

| Root word | Adjective – able or ible |
|-----------|--------------------------|
| value | |
| destruct | |
| enjoy | |
| remark | |
| notice | |
| knowledge | |
| pass | |
| reverse | |
| digest | |

## Activity 2

Choose the **-able** or **-ible** ending to complete each underlined word.

**a)** We had an incred_____ time at the zoo.

**b)** Look after that necklace please. It belonged to Gran and it is very valu_____.

**c)** I know that you like those shoes, but are they suit_____ for school?

**d)** Excuse me, is that table avail_____?

## Activity 3

Use the words from the list to complete the sentences below.

**incredible   audible   dependable   renewable**

**combustible   negligible**

**a)** Mr Brown has shown a solid and _____ personality.

**b)** The amount owing is _____; it's only a few pence.

**c)** The special effects in the movie were _____.

**d)** The wood will set on fire as it is _____.

**e)** _____ resources can be stored and used over and over again, for example solar and wind power.

**f)** She spoke so softly that she was barely _____.

## Investigate!

How many words can you think of in one minute that end with **able** or **ible**? Can you then add five more words that end in **able** or **ible**? Use the school library or the internet to help you.

# 4 Words ending in ant, ance and ancy

A word with the suffix **ant** will also take the suffixes **ance** and **ancy** if these forms of the word exist.

**important = importance**

The **ant**, **ance** and **ancy** suffixes are used after root words that can also have the **ation** ending.

**expect = expectation = expectant**
**tolerate = tolerance**

## Activity 1

Look at the verbs and nouns. Copy the table into your book and write the **ant** adjectives.

| Verb | Noun | Adjective |
| --- | --- | --- |
| hesitate | hesitation | |
| dominate | domination | |
| jubilate | jubilation | |
| stagnate | stagnation | |
| observe | observation | |
| tolerate | tolerance | |
| ignore | ignorance | |
| abound | abundance | |
| resound | resonance | |

## Activity 2

Put each of the words below into a sentence.

| | |
| --- | --- |
| truancy | fragrance |
| blatant | tolerant |
| hesitant | relevant |
| infancy | tyrant |

## Activity 3

These sentences all have two gaps. Choose the correct word from each pair to fill each gap. Use each word only once.

**a)** My _____ is completely _____ on me.
(dependent/dependant)

**b)** We need an _____ to be in _____. (attendance/attendant)

**c)** We've had _____ with the _____.
(correspondence/respondent)

**d)** My best friend is _____ that I can keep a secret; she tells me everything in _____. (confidence/confident)

**e)** The _____ in the case is speaking in his own _____.
(defendant/defence)

## Activity 4

Use the correct word from the list to complete each of the sentences below.

**hesitant    inhabitant    assistant**

**deodorant    defendant    accountant    occupant**

**a)** I have an _____ to do my tax forms.

**b)** The shop _____ was unhelpful and rude.

**c)** The _____ pleaded not guilty.

**d)** _____ keeps you smelling fresh!

**e)** His response to the teacher's question was very _____.

**f)** The next-door house has a new _____.

**g)** The island only had one _____.

## Investigate!

How many words can you find that end in **ant, ancy, ance**. Use these words to create a wordsearch for a friend to complete.

# 5 Words ending in ent, ence and ency

A word with the suffix **ent** will also take the suffixes **ence** and **ency** if these forms of word exist.

**evident = evidence**

The **ent**, **ence** and **ency** suffixes are used with words that have the following sounds:

*soft c* **decency**

*soft g* **urgent**

*qu* **frequency**

## Activity 1

Copy the table into your book and write the **ent** adjectives.

| Verb | Noun | Adjective |
|------|------|-----------|
| obey | obedience | |
| confide | confidence | |
| adhere | adherence | |
| cohere | coherence | |
| converge | convergence | |
| diverge | divergence | |
| emerge | emergence | |

## Activity 2

Add **ance** or **ence** to complete the words below.

reluct_____       insol_____       innoc_____

eleg_____       fragr_____       recurr_____

differ_____       pres_____       arrog_____

const_____       attend_____       prud_____

pati_____       dilig_____       assist_____

reli_____       repugn_____       excell_____

## Activity 3

Use the words from the list to complete the sentences below.

agency     complacency     decency     fluency

frequency     consistency     efficiency     absorbency

a) The sponge had a high level of _____.

b) She worked for a government _____.

c) You shouldn't approach anything with _____.

d) John mixed the ingredients into a creamy _____.

e) Saying sorry is a matter of _____.

f) The factory improved its _____.

g) She spoke French with great _____.

h) Radio waves have a lower _____
   than visible light.

Bonjour!

## Activity 4

Write the definition for each of these words. Use a dictionary to help you.

a) innocent _____

b) dependent _____

c) obedient _____

d) confident _____

e) independent _____

f) frequent _____

g) impudent _____

h) decent _____

## Investigate!

Look at the words you have created in Activity 4. Can you find the definition for ten of these words using a dictionary?

# 6 Suffixes: ery, ory and ary

There are three ways of spelling the 'ery' sound of this suffix -**ery**, -**ory** and -**ary**. Here are some ways that you might be able to remember:

| -ery | -ory | -ary |
|---|---|---|
| Usually nouns. However, some adjectives end with this suffix too. | Range of nouns, names of places and adjectives. | Range of nouns and adjectives. |
| scenery | story | library |
| stationery | glory | necessary |
| bakery | category | boundary |
| crockery | history | diary |
| battery | directory | dictionary |
| nursery | victory | illusionary |
| slavery | satisfactory | military |
| gallery | conservatory | quandary |
| cemetery | offertory | stationary |

## Activity 1

Choose the correct spelling of each of these words.

a) dictionary    dictionery    dictionory _dictionary_

b) necessery    necessary    necessory _necessery_

c) confirmatery    confirmatory    confirmatary _confirmatory_

d) artory    artery    artary _artory_

e) extraordinery    extraordinory    extraordinary _extraordinary_

f) honorary    honorery    honorory _honorery_

g) slippery    slippory    slippary _slipper_

## Activity 2

Use the clues to work out the missing **ery**, **ory** and **ary** words.

**a)** Where bread is sold: b _ackery_

**b)** Someone who takes notes: s _____

**c)** You choose to do this: v _____

**d)** A place or area: t _____

**e)** A subject in school: h _____

**f)** Where beer is made: b _____

**g)** For a short time: t _____

## Activity 3

Fill in the gaps with **ery**, **ory** and **ary** words to complete the sentences.

**a)** Children under five go to a _____; over five, they go to a
_____ school.

**b)** The first month is _____; the second month is _____.

**c)** Letters and envelopes are _____; a car that is standing still is
_____.

**d)** If you have to do it, it's _____; if you can choose, it's
_____.

**e)** Monks live in a _____; dead people are buried in a _____.

## Investigate!

How many words can you write down in two minutes ending with **ery**, **ory**, **ary**? Use these words to create anagrams for your friends to solve. Can you find some exceptions to the rule?

# 7 Adding suffixes beginning with vowel letters to words ending in fer

The suffixes **ed** and **ing** both begin with a vowel. When adding these suffixes to words ending in **fer**, there are two rules to follow.

- The **r** is doubled if the **fer** in the root word is still stressed when the ending is added.

  refer ⟶ referred

- The **r** is not doubled if the **fer** is no longer stressed when the ending is added.

  offer ⟶ offered

- This rule may be applied to other suffixes starting with a vowel.

  refer ⟶ referring

## Activity 1

Copy the table into your book and add **ed** and **ing** suffixes to each of the root words. Use the spelling rules above to decide whether or not to double the **r**.

| Root word | ed | ing |
|---|---|---|
| refer | | |
| prefer | | |
| buffer | | |
| differ | | |
| transfer | | |
| offer | | |

## Activity 2

Copy the table into your book and complete the words using the spelling rules.

| Root word | Suffix | Word created |
|---|---|---|
| infer | ed | |
| infer | ing | |
| refer | ee | |
| prefer | ence | |
| suffer | ing | |
| suffer | ed | |
| tranfer | ence | |
| refer | al | |

## Activity 3

Choose the correct word to complete each of the sentences below.

**transfer refer offer referred prefer reference
transferred referee offering preference referral**

**a)** The players surrounded the _____ when he blew the final whistle.

**b)** Please can you _____ to your homework planner in this lesson.

**c)** I tried to find the answer in the _____ section of the library.

**d)** We have made you a decent _____ and we hope that you will accept it.

**e)** My new friend is from America; she _____ to our school last week.

**f)** My sister will eat that meal but it is not her _____.

**g)** Jack tried and tried but he couldn't wash the cartoon _____ off his arm!

**h)** I was delighted when she _____ to me as 'the boss'!

**i)** Do you _____ the violin or the recorder?

**j)** The doctor is going to make a _____ to a specialist about Dad's leg.

**k)** There will be a small collection at the end of assembly as an _____ to local charities.

## Investigate!

Use ten of the words from this unit to create a wordsearch for your friends to complete.

Can you teach a friend the rules for adding **ed** or **ing** to words ending in **fer**?

# 8  Using a hyphen

A hyphen is often used to join two or more words that together form an adjective. This is called a **compound adjective**.

**The well-known author.**

**The police made house-to-house enquiries.**

A hyphen is sometimes used to join a prefix ending in a vowel letter to a root word that starts with a vowel letter.

**re-enter, pre-exist, de-ice**

Hyphens are also used when numbers are spelled out.

**sixty-five, two-thirds**

Notice that a hyphen is shorter than a dash.

## Activity 1

Rewrite the underlined words in the sentences below, using hyphens.

a) The burglar was caught <u>redhanded</u>. _____

b) It was an old <u>reel to reel</u> tape. _____

c) The plant had <u>yellowish green</u> leaves. _____

d) They lived in a <u>rent free</u> cottage over the summer. _____

e) The box was made of a <u>heavy duty</u> plastic. _____

f) They had a <u>heart to heart</u> conversation. _____

## Activity 2

Match the words to make hyphenated compound words. Write the words.

a) slow            footed

b) good            looking

c) flat            bottom

d) rock            hearted

e) broken          witted

## Activity 3

Insert hyphens to make the sentences below correct. There may be more than one hyphen in each sentence.

**a)** Unfortunately, the unlucky beetle was half alive when we discovered him in the back garden.

**b)** My mythical beast is half man, half spider and six legged.

**c)** There is three quarters of a pizza left, half a chicken and one quarter of a tub of ice cream.

**d)** Would you like a sugar free lolly or a tasty, delicious and healthy bag of grapes?

## Activity 4

Use each of these words correctly in a sentence.

**a)** cold-blooded

**b)** custom-built

**c)** hair-raising

**d)** eye-opener

**e)** re-formed

**f)** co-owner

## Investigate!

How many words can you find around the classroom, in the school library or on the internet that use a hyphen?

Can you explain the difference between the following words?

**left-hand** and **left hand**

**cold-blooded** and **cold blooded**

# 9  The 'i before e except after c' rule

For the ee sound that is common in English words, there is a spelling rule that says 'i before e except after c'. Here are some example words.

| i before e | Except after c | Exceptions |
|---|---|---|
| handkerchief | ceiling | seize |
| relief | deceive, deceit | protein |
| belief | conceive, conceit | caffeine |
| siege | receive, receipt | |
| piece | perceive | |
| niece | | |
| shield | | |

When the letter combination **ie** or **ei** do not make the ee sound, there are more variations, for example **neighbour**.

| ie as long sound *i* | ie sounded as two syllables | ei as *ay* sound | ei as *ai* sound |
|---|---|---|---|
| lie | science | vein | their |
| die | glacier | veil | heir |
| pie | happier | rein | |
| tie | quiet | reign | |
| tied | fiery | weight | |
| ties | | eight | |

## Activity 1

Look at the following words. Choose the correct spelling.

**a)** their   thier   _____

**b)** recieved   received   _____

**c)** weight   wieght   _____

**d)** deceitful   decietful   _____

**e)** chief   cheif   _____

**f)** thief   theif   _____

## Activity 2

Complete the sentences below. All of the missing words contain either **ie** or **ei** spellings.

**a)** Somebody who steals is a __ __ __ __ __.

**b)** I am not lying! Don't you __ __ __ __ __ __ __ me?

**c)** You are given a __ __ __ __ __ __ __ when you buy something from a shop.

**d)** Father Christmas rides on a __ __ __ __ __ __.

**e)** The girl who thought she was beautiful and was always looking in the mirror was __ __ __ __ __ __ __ __ __.

**f)** You need to be a certain __ __ __ __ __ __ to be able to go on that fair ride.

## Activity 3

Choose the correct word to complete each sentence below.

**receive     ceiling     fierce     receipt     mischief**

**obedient     believe     shrieked     deceive**

**a)** "Help, help!" _____ the toddler as he fell from his bike.

**b)** Do you know where the _____ is for the jeans that you bought last week?

**c)** Dad decided to paint the _____ in the bathroom.

**d)** I cannot _____ you have caused so much _____ in school today.

**e)** After three weeks of training, our puppy is much more _____.

**f)** Did you _____ the invitation to our party?

**g)** What a _____ voice she has!

**h)** The villain in the book managed to _____ everybody!

# 10 Homophones and near-homophones

As you learned in Year 5, homophones are words that sound very similar but are spelled differently and mean different things.

**aloud** and **allowed**

A near-homophone is two words that sound very similar, but are spelled differently.

**peas** and **peace**

## Activity 1

Choose the correct homophone to complete each sentence.

**a)** Last _____, I went for a walk in the moonlight. (knight/night)

**b)** _____ is my favourite colour. (blue/blew)

**c)** If you want to go on holiday, you may have to catch a _____. (plane/plain)

**d)** I comb my _____ every day. (hair/hare)

**e)** Bernard got mud on his _____ shoes. (new/knew)

**f)** I'm over _____! (hear/here)

**g)** Sherelle is hiding over _____. (they're/there/their)

**h)** Suzanne scraped her knee and now it's really _____. (saw/sore)

## Activity 2

Write the following passage into your book with the correct homophones. You will need to change **19** spellings.

Do ewe think that you can spot all of my errors? Please reed my work as their are sum deliberate mistakes. I taught eye had corrected all of them butt I now realise I should have spent moor thyme. I was write to ask for your help because I no ewe will bee able to fix the mistakes quickly. I hope and prey that they're are not to many. Please do not weight for me to start; you don't knead anymore advise from me.

## Activity 3

Some nouns and verbs are often confused because they sound the same or very similar. They are called **near-homophones**.

**drawer** = a storage compartment    **draw** = to illustrate something

Copy the table into your book. Write definitions for these noun and verb pairs that sound very similar.

| Noun | Verb |
|---|---|
| breath | breathe |
|  |  |
| ceiling | sealing |
|  |  |
| device | devise |
|  |  |
| effect | affect |
|  |  |
| lesson | lessen |
|  |  |

## Investigate!

How many common homophones can you find? Write a list that will help you with your writing. An example could be **their**, **there** and **they're**.

# 11 Etymology and word families

Words in a word family often share a common root word, but are also related by grammar or meaning.

**cent, centipede, century, percent, centenary**

The root word is **cent** – meaning one hundred.

## Activity 1

Choose the two words in each group that belong to the same word family.

**a)** write     sign     book     signature     stencil

_____     _____

**b)** employ     conform     employment     triangle     unicorn

_____     _____

**c)** bicycle     judge     binary     uniform     aerobics

_____     _____

**d)** decade     universal     decagon     formation     deliver

_____     _____

**e)** miniature     terrain     minimum     percent     aquatic

_____     _____

**f)** antibiotic     sympathy     biography     reform     mythology

_____     _____

## Activity 2

Add three more words to each word family.

**appear**            **graph**            **family**

_____    _____    _____

_____    _____    _____

_____    _____    _____

## Activity 3

Copy and complete the family trees for the root words **bitter** and **cross** by finding words that belong to each word's different word families.

<u>Form:</u> Add other nouns, verbs, adjectives or adverbs that are related.

<u>Spelling:</u> Add words that share a spelling with, or contain, the original word.

<u>Meaning:</u> Add words that share the meaning, including synonyms and antonyms.

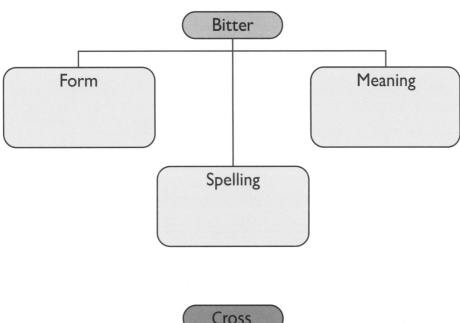

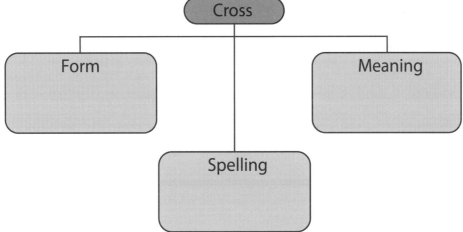

## Investigate!

Can you think of two other words where you could create a word family tree?

# 12 Irregular word spellings

Some words are difficult to spell because they are not spelled like they sound. The word **said** rhymes with **led** and **fed** but is spelled very differently.

The only way to remember irregular spellings is to learn them. However, there are ways to do this other than just staring at the words. There are different strategies we can use to try to remember these words.

| Strategy | Method | Words to try |
|---|---|---|
| Look, Say, Cover, Write, Check | Look at the word, say it out loud, cover it up, write it out and then check it. | tongue t-o-n-g-u-e<br>ocean o-c-e-a-n<br>disguise d-i-s-g-u-i-s-e<br>asthma a-s-t-h-m-a |
| What's The Problem? | Look at the word. What makes it so different? Underline or highlight the part of the word that is difficult. | leopard<br>restaurant<br>twelfth |
| Speak Differently | If a word isn't written how it sounds, say it out loud and pronounce it so that it *does* match the spelling. | definitely<br>Wednesday<br>particularly |
| Words Within Words | Look for smaller words in longer words. Visualise these smaller words with pictures to make it easier to spell the longer words. | There is a **rat** in sepa**rat**e. |
| Silly Saying  | Make up a rhyme to help you remember how to spell a word.<br><br>because = **b**ig **e**lephants **c**an't **a**lways **u**nderstand **s**mall **e**lephants | rhythm<br>necessary<br>arithmetic<br>geography<br>argument<br>ocean |

## Activity 1

Circle the correct spelling of each of these words.

**a)** enuff     enouff     enough

**b)** straight     streight     striaght

**c)** guarante     guarantee     garentee

**d)** heght     height     hieght

**e)** beginning     begining     biginning

**f)** skhool     school     scool

**g)** faroh     pharaoh     faraoh

**h)** werd     weard     weird

## Activity 2

Copy this piece of writing into your book and correct the spelling mistakes.

When they reeched France, they were pakked into trians, which stoppped and startd and crawld all day along the overcrowded tracks.

The country didn't look so diferent. Pepole worked the feilds just as the lads had done bac home. Some of the workeers unbent their backs and waveed as the trayns went bye.

The solidiers finaly arived at a small stasion that had grown into a vast suply depot. Trains and trucks were being shuntted and unloaded. Moutains of stores, horse lines and mule liens were evrywhere and ther was a bable of shoutd commands.

Then, at lsat, they were of the trains and marching. Will feltgod to bee out in the fresh air and swinging allong with his maets.

## Investigate!

Which spelling rules do you use the most? Use two other spelling rules from the list that will help you remember irregular words.

Think of ten irregular words and use them to create a crossword.

# 13 Proofreading

When you write a sentence, paragraph or essay, it is important that you re-read your work and check for any mistakes. We call this proofreading. There are a number of different types of error you should look out for.

- **Spelling**: Check difficult-to-spell words and words you know quite well but may have made a careless mistake with.

- **Punctuation**: Check you have punctuated your writing correctly, using full stops and capital letters. Also check the following.

  - Make sure you haven't used a capital letter after a comma (unless the word after the comma is a proper noun).

    - **We went shopping, Which was really tiring.** ⟶ **We went shopping, which was really tiring.**

  - **Apostrophes**: Make sure you haven't made mistakes with apostrophes.
    - **its** instead of **it's** or vice versa
    - **wont** instead of **won't**
    - **childrens'** instead of **children's**

  - **Homophones**: Check to make sure you haven't used the wrong word.
    - **your** instead of **you're**
    - **there** instead of **their**
    - **alot** when you really mean **a lot** (there's no such word as **alot**!)
    - **draw** instead of **drawer**

## Activity 1

Copy the following passage into your book and correct the ten punctuation errors.

Its really very im-portant to re-read your Own writing and check that it makes sense You must reMember to use the correct punctuation marks. When, you, are punctuating direct speech, use inverted commas around what the person is saying and ensure that all other punctuation (commas, exclamation marks question marks and full stops are inside the inverted commas,

## Activity 2

First identify the types of mistakes in the passage, then copy out the passage into your book and correct the mistakes.

Russell groaned his mum shouted up the stairs; "Russell, get up now or you'll be late – again!"

"Riiiight." he called back wearily. "It's always same," he thought "just when you were warm, comfy and having a fabulous dre – what was that?" Russell's train of thought was interrupted by a small figure running along the top of the skirting boards. It was only there for a second, but he was sure he'd seen. Russell shook his head in an effort to 'reboot' his vision. But no, there it was again, this time climbing up the leg his desk. A small person, no more than six inches high, scaling the telegraph pole sized upright.

Russell felt no fear, only curiosity. It occurred to him that maybe he was a) dreaming or b) going slightly mad but he decided that having imp or a pixie in his room was far more interesting than getting dressed, whatever the reason for its appearance. He approached slowly, much like when he was trying to catch his rabbit to put it to bed, "'Mustn't spook it." He whispered himself.

"Oi, who are you calling it?" said a tiny voice.

## Activity 3

Insert commas in the following sentences to ensure that they are correct.

a) I really enjoy swimming horse riding and cricket.

b) For PE you will need: jogging bottoms a sweatshirt a water bottle and a suitable pair of trainers.

c) My little brother also known as Annoying Albert gets on my nerves!

d) Before he knew it the clock struck 12 and it was time to depart.

e) The restaurant which was called Aqua served the most amazing charcoal grilled dishes!

## Investigate!

Proofread your last piece of writing using the list of common errors given in this unit. Make changes to your writing using a different coloured pen.

# 14 Word lists

These are some of the words that you are expected to understand and be able to spell correctly in Year 6.

| | | |
|---|---|---|
| according | develop | individual |
| amateur | equipment | interfere |
| attached | especially | interrupt |
| average | excellent | language |
| awkward | existence | leisure |
| bargain | forty | lightning |
| cemetery | frequently | mischievous |
| controversy | guarantee | muscle |
| convenience | harass | prejudice |
| criticise | hindrance | unnecessary |
| curiosity | identify | sacrifice |
| determined | immediately | sincerely |

## Activity 1

Circle the correct spelling of each of these words.

**a)** haras    harrass    harass _____

**b)** occupy    occupie    ocupy _____

**c)** stomack    stomac    stomach _____

**d)** achieeve    achieve    acheive _____

**e)** professhun    professian    profession _____

**f)** reconise    recognyse    recognise _____

**g)** community    communitey    comunity _____

**h)** pregidice    prejudice    prejudise _____

## Activity 2

Use each of these words in a sentence to show its meaning.

a) signature _____

b) recommend _____

c) according _____

d) privilege _____

e) persuade _____

## Activity 3

Practise writing and spelling the following words.

| Write | Look  Cover  Say  Check |
|-------|--------------------------|
| frequently | |
| guarantee | |
| lightning | |
| mischievous | |
| convenience | |
| community | |
| persuade | |

## Investigate!

Can you add the prefix **dis**, **mis** and **re** to some of the Year 6 words?

Can you add the suffix **ate**, **ify**, **ed** and **ing** to some of the Year 6 words?

Can you change some of the Year 6 words from singular to plural?

# 15 Using a thesaurus

A thesaurus is a book of synonyms. It contains words in alphabetical order, each with a list of different words that mean the same or a similar thing. We can look up words in a thesaurus to make our writing more interesting.

The boy <u>ran</u> home as fast as he could.

The boy <u>dashed</u> home as fast as he could.

## Activity 1

Find other words that have a similar meaning to each of these words.

**a)** said          **d)** jump

**b)** walk          **e)** look

**c)** eat           **f)** smile

## Activity 2

Use a dictionary or a thesaurus and insert words into the spaces below. Be as creative as you can.

Suddenly the two children felt their feet _____ off the ground, the air _____ through their hair and they realised that they were indeed _____ into the sky! Where could they be heading? "This is rather _____" whispered the younger of the children.

Before they knew it, they were actually flying over _____. Beneath their feet they could see _____ in the fields, _____ in the streets and _____ next to them in the sky. What a bizarre Sunday afternoon we are having they thought!

No sooner had they had that thought, they began to _____ towards the landing pad. But this area looked different. _____ yet different. Everything looked slightly distorted, one might even say topsy-turvy. It was a land that was indescribable. Was that really _____? Were they actually _____? Even in their wildest dreams, they had never imagined a land made from _____, called _____!

Use a thesaurus to find a new word to replace each <u>underlined</u> word in the sentences below.

**a)** Stephen <u>hesitated</u> as he approached the edge of the ledge. _____

**b)** The rabbits <u>retreated</u> as they saw the lights from the car. _____

**c)** Her instructions were difficult to follow as they were very <u>vague</u>. _____

**d)** My younger sister can sometimes be very <u>petulant</u>! _____

**e)** It's such a shame that the view is <u>dreary</u>. _____

**f)** I wish we had more opportunities to be <u>spontaneous</u> at school. _____

**g)** The guest speaker has such a <u>monotonous</u> voice. _____

## Investigate!

Use a thesaurus to change five words in your last piece of extended writing. Underline these words and write the new words in a different coloured pen.

# 6 Synonyms and antonyms

Synonyms are words that have the same or similar meaning. Antonyms are words that mean the opposite of another word. Most synonyms do not mean exactly the same, and antonyms are not always exact opposites – there are shades of meaning between words.

To make your writing more interesting, try to build a larger vocabulary. It's good to think of different, more unusual words to use. A thesaurus is a useful tool for finding synonyms and antonyms.

## Activity 1

Match each word in the left-hand column and right-hand column to its synonym in the middle column. One has been done for you.

| hideous | drenched ———— saturated |
| nasty | ugly | gigantic |
| enormous | cross | furious |
| angry | delighted | horrible |
| happy | awful | joyful |
| soaked | huge | repulsive |

## Activity 2

Look at the words in the middle column of the table and then think of a synonym and an antonym for each word.

| Synonym | Word | Antonym |
|---------|-----------|---------|
|  | hot |  |
|  | over |  |
|  | dirty |  |
|  | near |  |
|  | laugh |  |
|  | different |  |
|  | loud |  |
|  | morning |  |

Read the following pairs of words and decide of they are synonyms (S) or antonyms (A).

**a)** lead, follow _____

**b)** genuine, sincere _____

**c)** abandon, discard _____

**d)** bluff, boast _____

**e)** anguish, sorrow _____

**f)** fail, accomplish _____

**g)** own, possess _____

**h)** demolish, repair _____

**i)** authentic, true _____

**j)** ignore, avoid _____

## Investigate!

Can you write two synonyms for each of these words using a thesaurus?

**spicy**

**answered**

**nervous**

**good**

**convince**

**bite**

# 7 Double negatives

Negatives are words that suggest there is no action or object. Examples of negative words are **can't, don't, won't, didn't, nobody, nothing, nowhere, unaware, undecided, incorrect**.

Two negatives together create a positive.

**I haven't seen nobody** means **I have seen somebody**. Here are some other examples of double negative statements.

**She wasn't unattractive.**

**The bed wasn't exactly uncomfortable.**

To remove a double negative, change one negative to a positive.

## Activity 1

Copy these sentences into your book and correct the double negative mistakes. The first sentence has been done for you.

**a)** I haven't got no money. I haven't got any money.

**b)** The hotel hasn't got not air conditioning.

**c)** The children didn't have no PE kits.

**d)** Paul said that the ball wasn't nowhere to be found.

**e)** I ain't got no time to do my homework.

**f)** The coach won't allow no more players on the team.

## Activity 2

Choose the correct word from the pair to complete the sentences.

**a) nothing/anything**

Jarek did not tell his father _____ about the accident.

Jarek told his father _____ about the accident.

**b) no/any**

There isn't _____ trifle left.

There is _____ trifle left.

## Activity 3

<u>Underline</u> the mistakes in this passage including negatives and double negatives.

Well, it's been a horrific day. I got in my car and the car hadn't got no engine! Luckily, my mum learned me to ride a bike! Well you know what the weather is like at the mo, it's right hot! I met my mate, Tim down the bottom of the road and we cycled along to work. Next thing, it was thunder what we heard! He didn't know nothing about what to do! I fell off my bike. I turned to Tim and said "It's OK, I don't want no help!"

Tim smiled and I laughed, he didn't know nothing about helping people.

We finally got to work and I told Kay the story, she laughed and said "He never!" when I told her about Tim cycling off and leaving me on the ground.

I sat down at my desk and Kay asked me about the big red book on my desk. I told her that my uncle gave me this book whenever I was born and he don't come visit me anymore!

My work involves doing some numeracy. It's funny really, at school I never got no sums right!

At 11 o'clock Kay brought round some cakes and I thought to myself "I'd like one of them cakes" and I haven't never seen a load of people jump out their chair quick enough to eat them.

I guess it wasn't that horrific really – I got cake!

## Activity 4

Copy this table into your book and underline the negative words in these sentences. Then tick the positive box if the meaning is positive (because of the double negative) or the negative box (because there is only one negative word).

| | Positive | Negative |
|---|---|---|
| The cat wasn't unaware of the mouse. | | |
| Space travel isn't without risk. | | |
| Beth has not understood the problem. | | |
| History is not totally clear about the fate of the king. | | |
| Nobody went nowhere. | | |

## Investigate!

Can you write five different double negative sentences?

# 18 Standard English

Standard English is formal English. There are many rules you must follow when writing in Standard English.

**Rule 1**: The words **I** and **me** must be used correctly.

**Rule 2**: The subject and verb must agree: **I was** (not **I were**).

**Rule 3**: Precise words should be used so that the vocabulary is technical and efficient.

**Rule 4**: Words should be written in full and no contractions or abbreviations should be used: **cannot** rather than **can't**.

**Rule 5**: Double negatives must be avoided.

**Rule 6**: A formal style should be used rather than a chatty, conversational style.

**Rule 7**: Relative pronouns should be used appropriately: **who**, **whom**, **which**, **whoever**, **whomever**, **whichever** and **that**.

## Activity 1

When you are writing in a formal style, you should avoid using contractions and abbreviations. Write these contractions out in full.

**a)** they're

**b)** shan't

**c)** won't

**d)** don't

**e)** I'll

**f)** shouldn't

**g)** we're

**h)** they've

## Activity 2

Write the meaning of these phrases in Standard English.

**a)** well good

**b)** shake a leg

**c)** sort of

**d)** best of both worlds

**e)** cross your fingers

**f)** put a sock in it

**g)** stretch your legs

## Activity 3

The meanings of some words change over time. Write a short definition to show both the traditional and modern meaning of each word below. One has been done for you.

| Word | Traditional definition | Modern definition |
|---|---|---|
| sick | ill, not feeling well | excellent, brilliant |
| cool | | |
| wicked | | |
| lame | | |
| tweet | | |
| wireless | | |

## Activity 4

Rewrite the following sentences using Standard English.

**a)** He learned me some skateboard tricks.

**b)** I ain't going out.

**c)** We was just playing football.

**d)** He should of took more care.

**e)** We was lucky not to get caught.

**f)** Give me one of them sweets.

**g)** That boy done good.

## Investigate!

Write a report about a theme of your choice. Use the rules for Standard English when writing the report.

# 19 Word meaning

It is important that in our writing we use words that are creative and thought provoking for the reader. However, we must ensure that we use the vocabulary in the correct context. Therefore, it is a good idea to use a dictionary to check the meaning of words we use less often, to ensure our sentences make sense when we use them.

## Activity 1

Can you find the word that is similar in meaning? Write it in your books.

a)

| minuscule | compact |
| --- | --- |
| | vast |
| | long-lasting |
| | similar |

b)

| substantial | slight |
| --- | --- |
| | gigantic |
| | reasonable |
| | clear |

c)

| sweltering | deceiving |
| --- | --- |
| | different |
| | freezing |
| | roasting |

d)

| vast | spacious |
| --- | --- |
| | little |
| | micro |
| | miniature |

## Activity 2

Choose another word with a similar meaning to replace the underlined word in each of the sentences below.

**a)** The sandwich looked <u>delicious</u>. _____

**b)** My sister is sitting on a <u>small</u> chair. _____

**c)** We had an <u>amazing</u> time playing in the final! _____

**d)** I don't know why but that house does look <u>scary</u>. _____

## Activity 3

Circle the word that is similar in meaning to each of these words.

**a)** abhor

    metal   hate   strong

**b)** enhance

    envelope   love   improve

**c)** tardy

    delicious   late   cold

**d)** blatant

    obvious   funny   scared

**e)** tedium

    boredom   freedom   fun

**f)** plummet

    fall down   a fruit   plumber

## Investigate!

Can you find five words in your reading book of which you are unsure of the meaning? Use a dictionary to find the real meaning of those words. When you are reading, jot down words you are unsure of to look up later.

# 20 Vocabulary in context

Often, you can figure out the meanings of new or unfamiliar **vocabulary** by paying attention to the surrounding language. **Context clues** are words or phrases in a sentence that help you work out the **meaning** of an unfamiliar word.

## Activity 1

Find one word that can complete both sentences in each of the pairs below.

**a)** After the show had finished, I stepped forward and took a _____.

She made a beautiful _____ out of ribbon to tie in her hair.

_____

**b)** Ouch! That ant just _____ me!

Would you like a little _____ of chocolate?

_____

**c)** I know that you are _____ to me!

I love _____ on the beach in the summer.

_____

**d)** I think you got a _____ share.

Are you going to the book _____ after school?

_____

**e)** Tomorrow should be a _____ day.

He was given a _____ for driving too fast.

_____

## Activity 2

The following words have more than one meaning. Write two sentences to show the two different meanings.

**a)** present

**b)** bark

**c)** brush

**d)** wound

**e)** produce

## Activity 3

Sometimes when you read an unfamiliar word, it can be difficult to define it. However, if you read around the word when it is in a context, we can use clues to help us. Use a dictionary to define each of the words below and write a sentence using them appropriately.

| Word | Definition | Sentence in a context |
| --- | --- | --- |
| esteemed | | |
| compromise | | |
| significance | | |
| provoke | | |
| abundant | | |
| humble | | |

## Investigate!

Can you find ten words with the same spelling but a different meaning, depending upon the sentence they are written in?

# Word lists

Here is a list of words you will need to be familiar with in Year 5. Some of them have tricky spellings which you will need to learn.

## unstressed vowels

(Year 5)

accommodate

bruise

category

cemetery

definite

desperate

dictionary

embarrass

environment

exaggerate

marvellous

nuisance

parliament

privilege

secretary

vegetable

## 'i' before 'e' except after 'c' when the sound is ee

(Year 6)

achieve

convenience

mischievous

## 'i' before 'e' only

(Year 5)

soldier

sufficient (exception to the rule)

variety

ancient (exception to the rule)

foreign (exception to the rule)

## double consonants

(Year 5)

accommodate

accompany

according

aggressive

apparent

appreciate

attached

committee

communicate

community

correspond

immediate

occupy

occur

opportunity

recommend

suggest

## suffixes and prefixes

(Year 6 review)

according

attached

criticise (criticise)

determined

equip(-ment, -ped)

especially

frequently

immediate(-ly)

(un)necessary

sincere(-ly)

## tion words

(Year 5)

competition

explanation

profession

pronunciation

## ough letter strings

(Year 5)

thorough

## word families

(Year 5)

familiar

identity

signature

symbol

(this is revision from Year 3)

## 'y' makes the 'i' as in *bin* sound

(Year 5)

physical

symbol

system

(this is revision from Year 3)

## 'c' makes *s* sound before 'i', 'e' and 'y'

(Year 6)

cemetery

convenience

criticise

excellent

existence

hindrance

necessary

prejudice

sacrifice

## ous words

(Year 5)

disastrous

## unstressed consonants

(Year 5)

government

## words originating from other countries

(Year 5 and 6)

conscience

conscious

desperate

yacht

## crosscurricular words

(Years 5 and 6)

forty

temperature

twelfth

## le words

(Year 5)

available

## other words

(Years 5 and 6)

amateur

average

awkward

bargain

controversy

curiosity

develop

forty

guarantee

harass

hindrance

identity

individual

interfere

interrupt

language

leisure

lightning

muscle

neighbour

persuade

programme

queue

recognise

relevant

restaurant

rhyme

rhythm

shoulder

signature

stomach

temperature

twelfth

vegetable

vehicle

yacht